# SHARDS

# shards

William Bortz

Printed in the United States of America
First Printing, 2018
ISBN 1979203377
Formatting, artwork, and photography by Greg Rudolph —
dogspitcreative.com

*to my sunflower*

*table of contents*

—

perspective ........................................ 8

kindergarten ...................................... 9

there is a wind that blows ................... 10

wire................................................... 11

weightless ......................................... 12

immortal............................................ 13

spite .................................................. 14

in coping............................................ 15

i ........................................................ 16

garden ............................................... 17

migrate.............................................. 18

—

far off honey...................................... 22

imagination........................................ 23

last one.............................................. 24

all just the same................................. 25

american dream.................................. 26

foster ................................................ 27

one pale face...................................... 29

lessons............................................... 30

cubicle ............................................... 31

—

love and summer ............................... 34

and which can.................................... 35

home.................................................. 36

guidance ............................................ 37

how simple it is ................................. 38

ii ....................................................... 40

clarity ................................................ 41

iii....................................................... 42

where it begins................................... 43

rubble ............................................... 44

—

iv ...................................................... 47

only at night...................................... 48

bruises............................................... 49

backslid ............................................. 50

ghosts ............................................... 52

char................................................... 53

in understanding.................................... 54
wolvves................................................. 55
v........................................................... 56
war....................................................... 57

—

untidy.................................................. 60
gravves ................................................ 61
in orbit, in essence ............................. 62
vi.......................................................... 63
remain.................................................. 64
content................................................. 66
olive branch......................................... 67
stars..................................................... 68
when l wasn't worth it......................... 69
shards................................................... 70
in the light........................................... 72
gravel.................................................... 73
vii......................................................... 74
lighthouse............................................ 76
undone ................................................. 77

—

viii........................................................ 80
in healing............................................. 82
reminders ............................................ 83
early afternoon .................................... 84
ix ......................................................... 85
little storms.......................................... 86
first breath........................................... 87
summer of 2014 ................................... 88
axiom ................................................... 89
landscapes ........................................... 90
barefoot................................................ 91
x ........................................................... 92
mundane............................................... 93
tissue.................................................... 94
xi .......................................................... 95
pine....................................................... 96
parking garages.................................... 97
patriot .................................................. 98
xii.......................................................... 100

—

before summer left that year
it gave me a wet kiss
and my hair is still matted like dew soaked grass
and July is just another day at the carnival
dusk is patient and slow to leave,
sitting idly just below the crest of low hills
keeping the color in the clouds
from blushing red to scared blue
and every other color in between that can only
exist on ephemeral planes
I twirl their wispy ends around a stick
just to see how fleeting moments taste
like sickness, like plastic
my youth is a spilled beer
a stagnant puddle
stale by morning
and washed away by the clumsy hands
of a hot afternoon rain

*—perspective*

we are never as cold
as the hands stretching out
from the darkness
leading us
into the night

*—kindergarten*

I am a mold
a copy
of every hand that
has ever touched me
and all I can do—in love
is retain the vibrancy
and crease in every fingertip
that has ever made me glow

*—there is a wind that blows*

there is a wind that blows
it catches me crouching
—almost slithering
beyond a line I have not
dared but dream to cross
until this moment
and it is me
and the withering trees
left blinded
in a territory I believed
was entirely unseen
but there is a wind that blows
and seems to catch all
even the bits of dust
that clash and clamor
as my heart does.
in the darkest of lands
I do roam
far away from any light past's seen
and it remains just me
and the frolicking
of forlorn and whimsical leaves
unaware, as I once was
that there is a wind that blows
completely camouflaged
that brings even the
most well-fed, and
boasting
leaves
stranded, dumb
on the cold ground

*—wire*

I sometimes wonder how
I could be loved
me
just a bent wire frame
of a person, really
I am
a mess of frailty
so carefully put together
yet so incapable of keeping shape
or showing even the slightest sliver of strength
on my own

but I am loved

*—weightless*

I am comprised almost
entirely of milkyways
of billions and billions
of uncountable destinations
that I believed were entirely
alive and blooming but
discovered I had stumbled upon
their remnants, which looked a
lot like home but was
actually ethereal dust
I kept with me to show
all the places I called home
that called someplace else
home first
I wear them all and
I am weightless

*—immortal*

my mouth joins other
mouths—asking the
sea to quit trembling
so we can wash our
teeth with infinity
so our hands can stretch
and trickle down the curvature
of the horizon
and feel the darkness
without having to
remain in the
darkness

*—spite*

in all its grandeur
in spotted white
the sky rests easy
patiently awaiting
the cloak of night
how I long to love the same way
—in silence
not in spite

*—in coping*

the world and its many woes
are most easily managed
cradling a mug of coffee in one hand
and clasping my wife's with the other

*—i*

don't we see ourselves
in the big, black night
in the stars that have passed

in each and every thing
that once was
but is no longer
we see a piece
of our self

*—garden*

love is a hypethral garden
prosperous and vast
I am beginning to take steps valiantly
all while admiring each petal

—*migrate*

I don't know if these are the right
words to use, but
when I think of waking up with you
in the morning
I no longer have the urge to migrate,
whether it be to someplace warmer or colder
I don't mind staying for awhile

—

there are fields
lush and green
fielding birds and butterflies
fields where the grass is trimmed
and the cement is swept
there are no tears
shed in these fields
and no pinwheels spinning
like flags in a turbulent breeze
there is just stillness
a void
and there are
no names on the crosses
only numbers

*—far off honey*

I sit and count, in a midday sun,
my troubles and woes
the casted shadows of full limbs
and branches poking
through my kitchen window
and stretching down the wall
the blackened tips
of my weary fingers—
filing and sorting
sight encumbered within my head;
a cracked spectrum misguiding illustrious light
a cooling wind kisses the skin
pulled tight across my brow
taming the droplets of sweat
clawing their way down my cheek
figures and numbers of
all assorted pleasures
mark the words
whispered between slivers and slips
all while wispy, white clouds tickle and tease
the afternoon sky
a voice calls out—
cooing to me in my dreariness;
a sound of a babbling stream
oh, how I long for a taste
of that far off honey!
but the bees are buzzing;
and what is sweet
is only sweet
until after the bitter taste of worry
has fallen from my teeth

*—imagination*

there is proof
that the world is cruel
in every person
who went from using
their imagination for
painting sunny fields
and colored flowers
with their fingers
to standing at a ledge
imagining who would
truly miss them

*—last one*

like a cigarette
you were short-lived
unsatisfying
and left me
weaker than you
found me

*—all just the same*

be kind to yourself, little flower
for the sun shines the same
on each and every one of us
tiny or tall
in bloom
or hardly blossoming
light holds its gaze
and kisses our petals
all just
the same

*—american dream*

aren't we all specks of dust
simply hoping the sun
directs its stare and
gleams upon us
for even just a moment
before we find a cozy place
to settle

*—foster*

when I pray
I always hesitate because I want to address my
heavenly father
but I have nothing on earth to compare him too
like speaking in a vacant auditorium
it feels a lot like lying
I was never taught how to appreciate what I have
and how do you ask for more or better
when you haven't fallen in love with what you
currently call yours
society wants me to believe I am almost entirely full
that I am one right decision away from being utterly
satisfied with myself
in all honesty, I will probably splice together a brand
new me

every five or so years
after my skin has taken enough of a beating and
begins peeling like
old paint in the family home
that was never thought to be passed down
l am only as whole as the burial site of unspoken
words sitting moist
in my throat
l remain
in the pale sun
the whisper of morning
the clumsy exit of night
in the stillness of life as it is in the process of filling
its lungs
l am my father
here and not
leading but distant
now but not ever listening
with a cigarette hanging loosely from my lips
l will watch the night sneak out over me
and wrinkle out a prayer and follow the smoke
until it dissipates and believe
that the words made it home

*—grace*

do the stars know that
they continue to glimmer
once blown out—would that
change the way they hold the
vast black in their palms for
the last time—would they
prolong the departure and
allow the sky to sift a bit
further into their milky pores
can leaving ever be an act
as graceful as slowly
fading to
morning

*—one pale face*

I first saw the moon in your palm,
milk—kept together. a sea
not meant for swimming

since, it has fallen below
—something conceived and birthed
oh, how easily I drown in empty black

in a lot of ways I have never stopped
leaking. I find myself lighter than previous
nights. I find things I meant to keep

beneath my pillow. I only sleep on
rocks now. they engrave my temples
with hieroglyphics. I know it isn't

a moon, now, but a frown
I cannot pull down or see
differently. sorrow has but

one pale face

*—lessons*

my mother taught me how to love
not in long talks over dinner
but in stories about her youth
told through breaths of smoke
my mother showed me that love is hard
because we can't always see the parts of us
that ache and when we don't acknowledge our dark
we don't allow the light to permeate
my mother told me to love with all that I am
in my brokenness and wonder & in my weakness and sorrow
she always said that she could love me better and I still believe
that she could have
it is imperfect and human to love in the way that she did
with only fragments of incapabilities
spliced together with humility

this is the only way to love someone

*—cubicle*

beyond the polymer strips
separating a splintered
and slightly fragmented
sheet of glass
lie rows and rows
of flowers, trees and leftover
particles of sunbeams
l have seen it all
but only in my waking dreams
it tempts from my peripherals.
my fingers fidget
on unsteady tiles
—clack, clack, clack
repetitious rattling
renovating, with each
maddening tick—the stronghold
l am kept within
impenetrable walls, belaying
all and any form of
free thought
leaving just me and
my restless conscious
and l am left to wonder
and ponder and believe
—in my constraint the
blood of my veins
would be a nice shade
of color
on the wall to my left

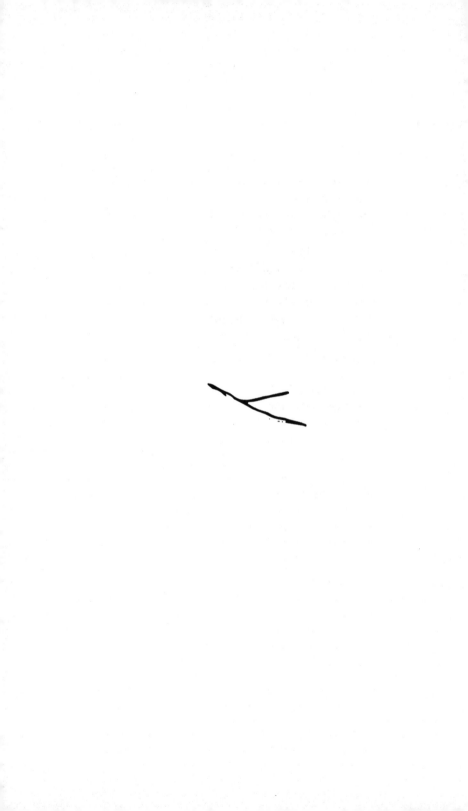

—

you are sad in the mornings because you think of
all the things you could potentially overlook.
you make sure to listen to the birds sing and write
poems to yourself, reflecting on the words of your
mother and father.
you watch the shadows pass over the pine needles
in the park and brush your fingers over the indents
left on the back of your legs by the cluster of them
that have fallen.
you drink in the sun before it falls below the
horizon. yet at night, that ache is as evident as
ever—having ignored not the day, but what it
conjured up inside of you.

*—love and summer*

in the heat of a midday July sun
I so easily forget the brutality of winter
just as in the midst of harmonious
relationships I forget
how easily I can become bitter
so quickly does that sharpness
sift into the soft parts of my bones
and I forget the warmth of love
and summer

*—and which can*

when I become lost
stumbling through the dark
that is where I discover
who I wish to become

but upon multiple periods
of full light
I cannot find my way back
to that better
fuller
person

and I pray
to never get
lost again
to never
get close to

finding my true
self again

because what an impossibility
to know which version of myself
cannot see clearly

*—home*

home is the first river
that washed me
that sent me out alone
that filled my veins with
a mighty current
—to not ever remain quiet
or still
to be fierce
to carve

I lie my head
on the bedrock of
necessary change
and become the strongest
thing that has ever been
so silent

*—guidance*

wind is the softest
thing that has ever
kept me from running
away
using
the loudest and most
delicate voice
to graciously remind
me that I cannot get
better alone
that I cannot heal
all by myself

*—how simple it is*

how my feet
would greatly appreciate
the rest
how thankful
my eyes would be
to close for a moment
maybe catch a
glimpse of sleep

the coffee has left
stains on the inside
of my eyelids
—brown puddles
of murky lake water
I could surely get lost in
and maybe there
find a piece of silence

what is there left to wonder
question or whimsically ponder
aside from where, oh, where
does the pavement end
I haven't felt the tickle
from a blade of wild grass
since I was but
a little seedling

even the clouds have
gone to bed
no one was around to
notice their slick escape

how simple it is
to wait around
just waiting
to topple over and die

*—ii*

maybe I cannot
feel the weight
of my sin
because the darkness
of my old life was
always in contrast to
that of the dim light
I lived in; I was not
being as bad as those
who motivated me to
'not end up like they did'

*—clarity*

so many times
I looked for answers
in a cup of coffee
and my hands got cold
well before I found clarity

then you intertwined
your slender fingers in mine
and taught me how to appreciate
that time late in the day
when the colors are fully alive—vibrant
and the air glides generously
across the water
and the world seems so
fragile that I am sure it may break apart
but your eyes catch mine
and all that exists
and all that has ever and will ever exist
sifts perfectly into place

*—iii*

o' night
pull me under
into a
chlorine moon
bath

please scrub the
most recent layer
of my skin away
because I have grown
terribly uncomfortable
in it

*—where it begins*

I'm far too eager to love, yet
not
prepared to forgive
myself for not knowing
what it means to be
full
and giving myself away anyway
I am exhausted
from continuing to fall asleep,
weighted down by
this stone heart of mine

*—rubble*

patience came when I
separated my touching palms
and let the rubble of the past
fall beneath my feet
—it allowed the present to quickly
fill and pour over
softening and cleansing
my trouble stained hands

—

I first met fear at the
age of twelve
it never swore or lashed out
it just crept into my heart
—gently shoving out love
convincing me to stay put
when I should have leapt
forcing me to be callous
when I should have wept
fear was novocain
for my restless soul
quietly pulling me
beneath raging waters.

*—only at night*

sometimes
I try so
hard
to immortalize
parts of me that
I have already
conquered, that I have
seen shudder out their
last wicked breath

*—bruises*

you tell me my flaws
fall so gently on your skin
when they leave bruises
on mine

*—iv*

as the road I am driving on
creeps to the left
and back to the right
down a slow curve
the small industrial park
finds its way into the background
the wispy plumes of smoke
overcome the light overcast sky
and I feel a sense of mourning
but I haven't lost a thing
I am reminded of being a young boy
and feeling the same sort of loss
without being able to carry
anything more than
what I would take
out to the playground at recess
—a great grieving
for something that I
cannot even understand
how to grasp

*—backslid*

last week I spoke to this kid
this man
who was the same age as I am
he was a few weeks into
his first bout with AA
and every breath of his
smelled sweet
like spring
—hopeful—
his words came out of his mouth
in the same way
spring flowers blossom
—proudly roaring back
into a hungry sky
I read today in the paper that
he
passed away

he was the same as
all of us; as me
and struggled with the same things
that all of us do
the root being
uncertainty
that drives us to the cusp
of darkness
even while we know all too well
what it is like to
see the ledge
crumbling rocks
and proudly walk away
sometimes
sometimes
a slight readjustment
trips us up
and drags us back
down
down

down

*—ghosts*

it isn't the things
I have failed at and destroyed
that both hinder my movement
and leave me stirring at night
it is the things I do not
really know of just yet
that I will surely fail at
that watch and cackle
in the darkness
from behind a partially
closed door

*—char*

every time someone tells
me I am kind or caring or
something similar
I cringe because I know
my heart and how
easily it
chars
and I know everyday is a struggle
to not fight every second
and more than that, most of
the time I give in to
the devil in
my bloodstream

*—in understanding*

your smallest breaths
those early morning gasps
—puffs of feathery clouds
freshly woke, stirring
to make it to
the beginning of the day
they get caught in my throat
not because they are coarse, no
but because they are
the first, light snowfall
on browned, dying ground
before I taste of
the sweetness that is
the essence of your life
I must first remind myself
what the spring feels like
what a rush of blood
does to the soul.
I must first remember
what it means to love
that which is not at all
deserving of love
before I can understand
the tender lay of your lips
upon mine—riddled with calloused rips

*—wolvves*

each day begins, rifle in hand
the foretaste of pine on my teeth
my bones undulating to the thumping
of an incessant war drum in my chest
for what is a better showing of strength
than appeasing the metal, chewing on the tension
and pulling the trigger to deaden the pressure

each day to end the same way
hand shielding the yawning rays of an exhausted sun
streams of iron running the length of my arm
yet, what I seek becomes the seeker
—radiating sight, gritted teeth, fermented growling—
just beyond the outstretched hand of light
and it is I who am being hunted
by that which through clenched fists demand

—*v*

l am trying my hardest
to see God in raindrops
to see the beauty
stuffed into the
cracks in the pavement
to see more than
my own reflection
in the windows l pass
l am just
really trying

*—war*

everything was a war to my father
doing the dishes, picking me up from school
putting down the beer, loving my mother
always clenching his fists
he got tired of shouting and left
leaving the blood to stain
my hands—passing on his war to me
fighting against everyone, ruthlessly
tearing apart enemies in my sleep
my father got tired
of fighting himself
so he gave that war
to me

—

I find that each step I take is a landmark in itself—
entirely worthy of its own praise. for I do not so
much remember the clearing I made it to, but the
leaves that brushed my face and the nettles that
pricked at my ankles. it is a grandiose picture of the
anatomy of succession; each movement being vital
and viewed in reverence.

*—untidy*

I am untidy
I am the first bite
of an early January morning
I am the raspy voice
in the still night
I am the sheets that cannot
stop me from sleepwalking
I am the hands that love
me
and there are far more
that keep me
than I will ever believe

*—gravves*

we spend our days
wishing and dreaming
yet it isn't until
we are lying
in our grave
that we begin
to claw towards
them

*—in orbit, in essence*

I do not have to convince
myself that I can keep the
sea in my palm with ease
I can maintain troubled waves
because I have held much more
turbulent bodies in
the panting spaces between

my fingers. I have taken
many breaths beyond the
moon. look at the stars
behind my ears. in the
space where nothing is
supposed to bloom collects

dew—in orbit, in essence
around a hollow moon. I have
found the end of numbers
counting each moment
between the breathing
of whom I dearly love
—and they have not yet

returned

*—vi*

in vibrant color
does the sun meet the night
and so must I
to each and every scowling voice
darkness hides

*—remain*

the winter's coming
brings with it a weight
that falls fully on my frame
—though I can support it,
it demands my cooperation
in not squirming as it nestles in
I do, with reserve
the cold makes me honest
it makes me aware of the
weariness that comes with
another season coming and going
—with another transition
that can be spent in introspection
of all that has begun to wither
within me

and how long I should let
it dangle before I decide to clip it
and myself be pruned
I constantly go back to the wilderness
to find strength
the rush of the collection
of fresh memories
from a past sun
just months ago—it shined,
still overflowing in my mind
I interrogate the trees
to try and uproot some wisdom
that the warmth burrowed
beneath their bark
but the cold has since exposed
leaving the strips of quiet wood
hanging
loosely against the biting wind
revealing nothing I don't already know
and what I purposely tucked away
will be marred by my inability
to stand and submit to the truth
that I, too, will be kissed
by the harsh winter air
again, and again, and again, and
I will do just
as they do
I will
remain

*—content*

I keep fire in my palm
a replacement for what I
want but cannot have
—for what I need but
do not want
and it seers
and I am consumed
chewed into ash
by an immeasurable
pile of dissatisfaction
and I burn atop
a kindling of unreachables

*—olive branch*

we missed it, I think
it flew right by our heads
barely brushing the new growth
on our cheeks. the bird with the burnt
branch in its mouth. the feline with the
half-living rabbit in its teeth

this pulsating plate of bone marrow
it is hungry for sex or blood
or how is it the difference is
being shared
especially to children who should not
know either intimately
but do because what a
battleground it is to be a youth
when you are born as ammunition
to be shot across a quiet field
or to be filled with spent powder

what a shame it is to be
half-alive and squirming or
a martyr burning but never
both at the same time

*—stars*

12am twilight
comes with a click
—a reset in my mind
a feeling of blossoming thought
built around a new day's arrival
another sunrise to warm my skin
another sunset to paint my dreams
with vivid color
maybe a touch of rain
and the croak
of heavenly trumpets
another batch of wonders
and wishes

*—when I wasn't worth it*

all l am trying to
say is that
l met the most
vile version of my-
self long ago
and made sure
he would never as
much as whisper a
sour wind in the
direction of the people
that saved me

*—shards*

for somewhere in between
the 24th and 36th time
you held two or three dozen
matte white pills in your hand
that would turn your already torn up insides
into much smaller shards
and I ask
do we learn love
from our mothers and fathers
or just our mother
or just our father
or from neither
or from careless strangers
*no*
it is a war we cannot run from
in our muscles and on our tongues
it's the breath between words
and the space between fingers
and the commitment
to leave those spaces open
for the day we meet a person
who sees the lessons as linear
instead of fragmented
—letting the light in
like slivers of sun
through dark clouds

the word—commit, is the essence of the promise
I gave to my wife
and the conclusion to the lifelong struggle
my mother had with the bitter berries in her palm

we voluntarily consume
more dark
than we are already
shrouded in
until we are full
and
at that point we
would rather cease
breathing
than fight our way
back
towards the
light

let alone
believe
it even exists
anymore

*—in the light*

I am the vase
I broke as a child
and couldn't take
responsibility for.
I am the floor it met
—entirely unmoved.
now I am the hands
carefully collecting
the fragments of myself
and admiring how their
sharp edges glimmer
in the light

*—gravel*

between the spinning, swirling grey of a blanketed sky
and the cracked and cooing cement beneath my feet
are paths marked with numbers I have not learned
to count up to just yet
troubled—I lack the understanding to see the difference
in molded alleyways, dripping with the hue of absent streetlight
and life-breathed creation of narrow walkways,
lined with berries and assorted fleeting blossomings
a commonly mislaid or too often negated
problem discomfort is; not in its longing to be corrected
but in the apathetic wonderment of thought—
with no clout to be squeaked out between breaths—
the wisdom needed for taking a step is certainly not found
in misplaced judgment—as tragically appropriate as it can be
but in the trust allocated to the twinge
of the muscles—eager to feel the shock of unleveled ground

*—vii*

I retain every version of myself that
has peeled away from the flesh in one flaky piece
I keep them in gold, in flecks, sunken
into the brown of my sleepless eyes
getting older equates to equal parts
remembering and equal parts forgetting
or repressing and dwelling either or
when I was really young I was terrified of storms
I would cower beneath flashes and fists
slamming on the trembling table-top of the sky
but now I love them and
I sit up on sticky summer nights
drinking in the debris from thunder-strikes
I hold the lightning in my teeth
for as long as I can handle the rattling
basically I don't know at what point
we decide to stay up all night
with the things we were once so scared of
when do we start to see fear
as a severe lack of light
instead of an abundance of darkness
when does courage seep into bone
my sister used to be absolutely terrified
of men with beards
she would howl at the sight of one
but now she is engaged and has
two beautiful boys with the most
lumberjack-looking-dude
you could imagine

I don't know at what point we decide
to settle down and start a life with what scares us
sometimes I think too much about being a kid
how everything was whimsical
even fear tasted sweet
how great it was to feel so small and
to believe everything was magical
everything eventually became dull and I began
emptying myself of wonder layer by layer
leaving bits of stardust on my fingertips
I miss being young
and what I mean when I say I miss being young
is I don't remember what it is like to believe in
infinity
all I know are endings and I am not sure
which ones to welcome and which to mourn
and mostly how do we discern between the
change we force and the growth
we desperately need
this life thing is sometimes such a sick sad
sham of a marriage and I am often wondering
who needs the other more
if I am being generous at the very least
I could say I am still very much in love with
all the scarlet evenings I spent time with
when I was hardly even aware I had done
any living yet
before the sky looked angry as it collapsed into
dusk
before I grew bored with it
before I realized how much of me it had swallowed

*—lighthouse*

her voice is what led
me to love her
especially in the dark
whispers like a cool breeze
long drawn-out syllables
exasperating her point
an object I could hold
and feel when things
were strange
and I needed comfort
or just warmth
or a lighthouse
guiding me safely
to shore

*—undone*

everything I know of could
be named a blade of
grass—undeserving of
both the sharpness and
politeness it could potentially
greet the tender skin of my feet with

I have all the teeth
I need but I have had more
it goes the same for the hands
whispering their softness
into my spine

a slow-creeping summer
swallows pockets of
chilled air. I once held
your breath in my unmoving
hallowed ground of a
mouth—as pure and brittle
as an unchanging wind

I will forever wonder
if I was meant to
remain in the cold
belly of my uncertain
mother and be

undone

—

of all the things
I can hold in my hands
and keep in my throat
you
are the most precious

*—viii*

I found her mid-bloom, strong and vibrant—
navigating the labyrinth of her youth with a quiet
confidence. she spoke to strangers with a type of
love I hadn't seen before—bridging murky and
anxious waters with an outstretched hand because
she knew she didn't have much to offer aside from
a kind word and an honest heart; and at the core of
her being, she believed that was all anybody truly
needed.

we loved like a mighty river flows: intently and
unforgivingly. every brushstroke of my lips to her
skin was part of something much larger. we spent
our first summer together in a cave of blankets,
gazing up at the stars we stuck on the ceiling above
my bed. our wish each time one loosened its grip
and fell was for time to stop, or at least slow a little,
because in those fleeting moments before our eyes
folded beneath the weight of sleep we would talk
about days to come—when the morning would no
longer linger on our tongues like fresh fruit.

she plucked a guitar in the same manner that unabashed children pull dandelions from their cozy soil bed. I told her so often, hands that soft are meant for holding, and holding onto for a long while. I sit in wonder—in turmoil, I ponder—and reflect on early summer afternoons spent somewhere, lost between my fantasy and your growing disdain. such a perfect place to trace the outline of your ribs with my fingertips, while following your blissful gaze to the birds soaring freely overhead. so free, you whispered and I echoed. you withered and wandered so far from home, and I heard it not in your words, but in your eroding voice.

it took you some time to learn that no one buries the birds that plummet out of the sky and onto the concrete; and that freedom is being caught, bandaged, and encouraged to pursue the clouds again. in my loneliness, I discovered my failure to nourish you properly. I plucked you when I should have watched you grow and flourish in the light of the sun. I shouldn't have tried to keep you. it was simply the reflex of an uncertain and doubtful heart. I know this now. our love has slowed to a gentle stream. we are patiently floating downstream, gliding around rocks and downed trees with the wisdom of seasoned sailors.

*—in healing*

I am learning to love
every piece of me

I am handling
all of my sharpest
edges

I am
healing

*—reminders*

—leave space
in your mouth for rain
behind your ears for flowers
in your twilight for fire
in between your fingers for fingers
in your hand for tomorrow

*—early afternoon*

some days
the world
seems content
with being silent
and I dare not disturb it
other days the only things
I feel that I need to say
are spoken softly into her mouth

*—ix*

in the way
she begins
so subtly
and floats along
with purpose and direction
—a confidence in simply being
with a departure
like the wispy tip
of a traveling cloud

she is a poem

*—little storms*

I love how small
your fingers are
and how they feel
in my palm—
little storms
I will fall asleep to
and as I drift away
they will rage

*they will rage*

*—first breath*

something I have longed for,
in the midst of my incessant dreaming;
a sound—a voice called back from within
the cluster of spirits—passed the ivory tombstones
wishing well to old spells; into the space
through which comets traverse—a blackness,
a waiting
falling out gracefully from your petals
of fantasy pink: my name, in kind lettering
against an angry sky
as if I haven't ever heard a sound; as if I hadn't breathed a
single breath
until you knew who I was—I hadn't lived

*—summer of 2014*

she settled into the warmth
of my silence
and we shared sighs
paired with the fluttering
of fingertips
until the weight of love
buried us
in a sea of blankets
we didn't struggle
or try
to reach the surface
we surrendered to sipping reality
between gulps of each other's breath
until twilight crept in on us
and never left

*—axiom*

your kiss is like
a mouthful of wine
as the wind
—in a fury—
hits a cluster of discarded autumn leaves
and the chill recedes
just before meeting my bones.
bliss

*—landscapes*

all those years
I spent looking
for landscapes
to fill in the background with
for something
to hold in my hands
and always coming
up short of fulfilled
make sense to me now.
I didn't need sunrises
and creek beds;
I didn't need coffee
or smoke breaks.
I needed your groggy
eyes at 6am
and your slender fingers
penning sonnets on our bed sheets
as we fell asleep
I was so lost
and so unsure
of where home was
until I found my reasons
and my comfort
inside of your chest

*—barefoot*

I have been many places
I have taken buses to bustling utopias
walked along the basin
of vast canyons
carved by patient rivers
I have felt the flickering lips of cruelty
and brushed against the softness of a kind word

in the small of your back
in the pockets between your fingers
in the secret garden behind your ears
I dream of your roots growing in
I dream of being the reason
the paint on your fingernails chips
even while my hands caress
the unstable curves and empty plains
—I am missing them
and cannot wait
to return again

*—x*

I love her
in the same way
the breeze
treats my skin—
with ease
and gentleness
without a forceful allure
but with an openness—
a longing to simply be felt
and an honesty
that to its depths
is warm

*—mundane*

I am lost in the fingerprints
smudged on the wall
and the empty plates and half-filled
coffee mugs littering the table.
incessant chatter spills out all around
—the smell of croissants following closely
my wife sits across from me,
talking about Europe and coffee
and about the stain on her white
& navy striped shirt.
I feel like the wide store-front window
or like the ceramic vase filled with
plastic flowers that stands guard
over the pile of used napkins;
there and not—but full in any case.

*—tissue*

that thin layer of film
between your bone and skin
is where I would like
to lie
gently pressed between
the canvas I love—
painted as soft
as an evening glow—
and my sturdy foundation:
what I have come
to know as home

*—xi*

for you, even the smallest gesture
—a small kiss as you exit through the door,
watching you sip sip sip away
at your brimming cup of tea,
or holding your hand at the market—
l will do with such a grave
degree of fervor.
and even the moon cannot help
but beat down on the shores
in the high quiet of night
just watching you sleep

*—pine*

in my bones
1 can feel it—
my love for her
placed firmly
into the rest of me
interlaced within
my ability to breathe
and the constant hum
calling me to create
since the formation
of my soul
1 have pined for her

*—parking garages*

there is something
beautiful in her—
I do not know
if it is the sunbeams
in her eyes
or the poorly lit
parking garages
of her heart,
maybe it is the shadows
stretching to show
on her skin
blooming into
freckles and imperfections
or just that
she dances in both
the light and the dark—
kissing the ground
thankful just to
be standing

*—patriot*

how great is my love of country
how badly I desire to fill all the fault lines
that embrace a faultless plain and do their best
to keep it from trembling
I was born in a bath of honey
every syllable I speak drips with unity
and I believe as a man of privilege
I cannot complain where it is I lay my head down
as long as there is a space for me to dream
and clouds above watching closely
for when I will be thirsting next
I know love is a landlocked country
because I have tried to fit the whole sea
in my mouth and cannot learn to
swim in the reservoir left over
love is the only place that has
ever told me I am welcome
even if it assures me I can never leave
it is the only place that feels like home
and I know I am home because the
sound I hear from my pressed ear to her chest
—that pitter-patter of her heartbeat—it is a parade
I can't say I am a pacifist because I believe war will come

and its call can't be ignored
l hope it isn't my hands that find all
the soft and weakening spots in your skin
—reach in and pull
but l probably will be more often than l would like
but as my duty
l will catch every drop in my mouth
l will keep them warm
l will not let them fall to the street and be cooked
into the concrete like a salt puddle
leaving the outline of someone innocent
we go home to the same
soil we were first washed in
l lick my lips and
taste the color of my continent
it takes an entire lifetime
or perhaps many
to paint a picture of
the landscape you will die on
at least one to learn how
to love every sprig
and brush of wood
and a few more to stay
a bit longer
and that is really all
l have to give

*—xii*

one day I decided
to take a step
and it hurt less
than standing still

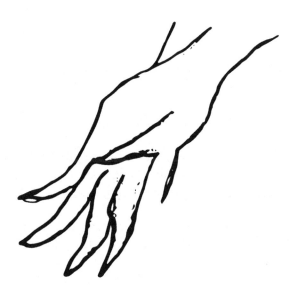

*acknowledgements*
———

to each and every person that ever invited me into
their home and into their family. I am greatly
indebted to you.

to my darling wife, who encourages and inspires me
every single day. I love you more than words could
ever display.

to my horizon line coffee family. thank you for the
support, love, friendship, and incredible coffee.

to Greg Rudolph. thank you for your wild brain and
talent, your brotherhood, your taste in cheap pizza
and beer, and for making this whole book come
together and look how it does.

to Casey Knue. thank you for being a stellar homie.

Made in the USA
Las Vegas, NV
01 October 2022